PRE-SCHOOL PRE-WRITING SKILLS

Fun-filled Activities

At The Slides!

Help the bunnies slide down. Trace the path.

Ferry Ride!

Giffy and Enny are on a ride across the sea! Trace the waves and clouds for them.

Cat Tails!

These cats with long tails have gathered tonight. Trace their tails.

There Hops The Frog!

Fredy wants to reach the toadstool. Trace the curves and help him reach there.

Curvy Path

Sizzly is happy to sail. Trace the curves as he moves through the water.

Trace the curves given below.

Bee Trails!

The bees are flying back home. Trace their trail.

Belly, The Curvy Butterfly

Belly is happy to see the flowers bloom. Trace the curves and complete the picture.

Trace the curves given below.

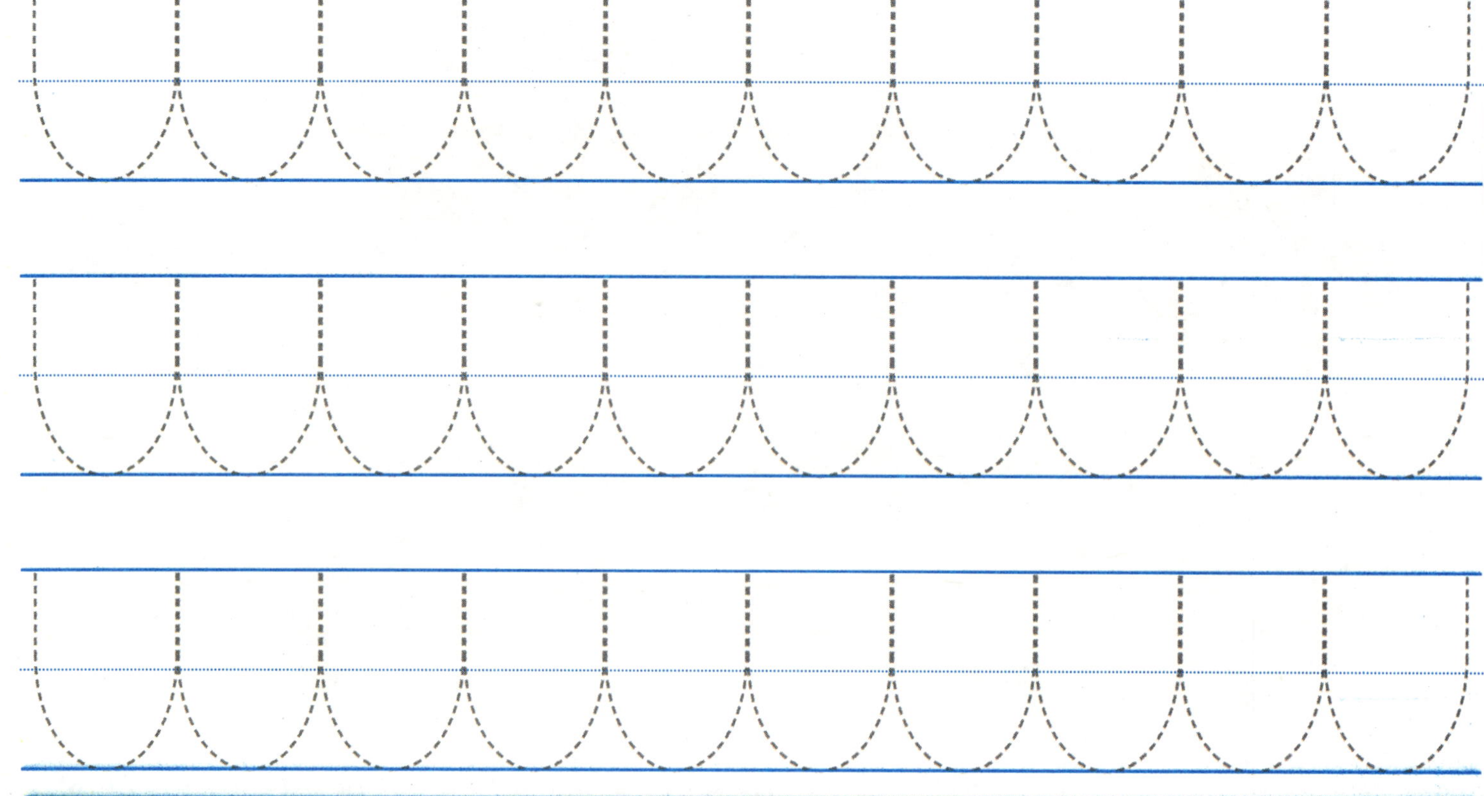

Off to Sleep!

It has started to snow. The penguin has to go to sleep! But where? Trace over the dots and complete the igloo for him.

Let's Take a Nap!

Miss Bee is taking a nap under the cap! Trace the mushroom for her and colour the picture.

Rat Race!

The rats are in a race! Trace the lines and help them reach the finish line.

Off We Go Left to Right!

Vroom goes the car! Trace the lines from left to right to complete the road.

Trace the lines given below.

Humpty Dumpty on a Wall

Humpty Dumpty is sitting on the wall! Trace the lines from top to bottom.

Jack on the Stalk

Jack is on the stalk. Help him climb down by tracing the lines from top to bottom.

Trace the lines given below.

By the Parachute!

The monkeys are landing! Trace the dotted lines.

Miss Cat with a Hat!

Miss Cat is getting ready for a party. To help her be on time, trace the lines on her hat.

Frog Prince in the Rain!

Complete the picture of the frog prince by tracing the slanting lines from left to right.

Trace the slanting lines given below.

To the Sky!

The witch is all set to fly! Trace the slanting lines from right to left. and complete the picture.

Trace the slanting lines given below.

Trace the Shapes

The shapes are here to meet you! Trace the dotted lines and complete these shapes. Say the name of the shape while you trace.

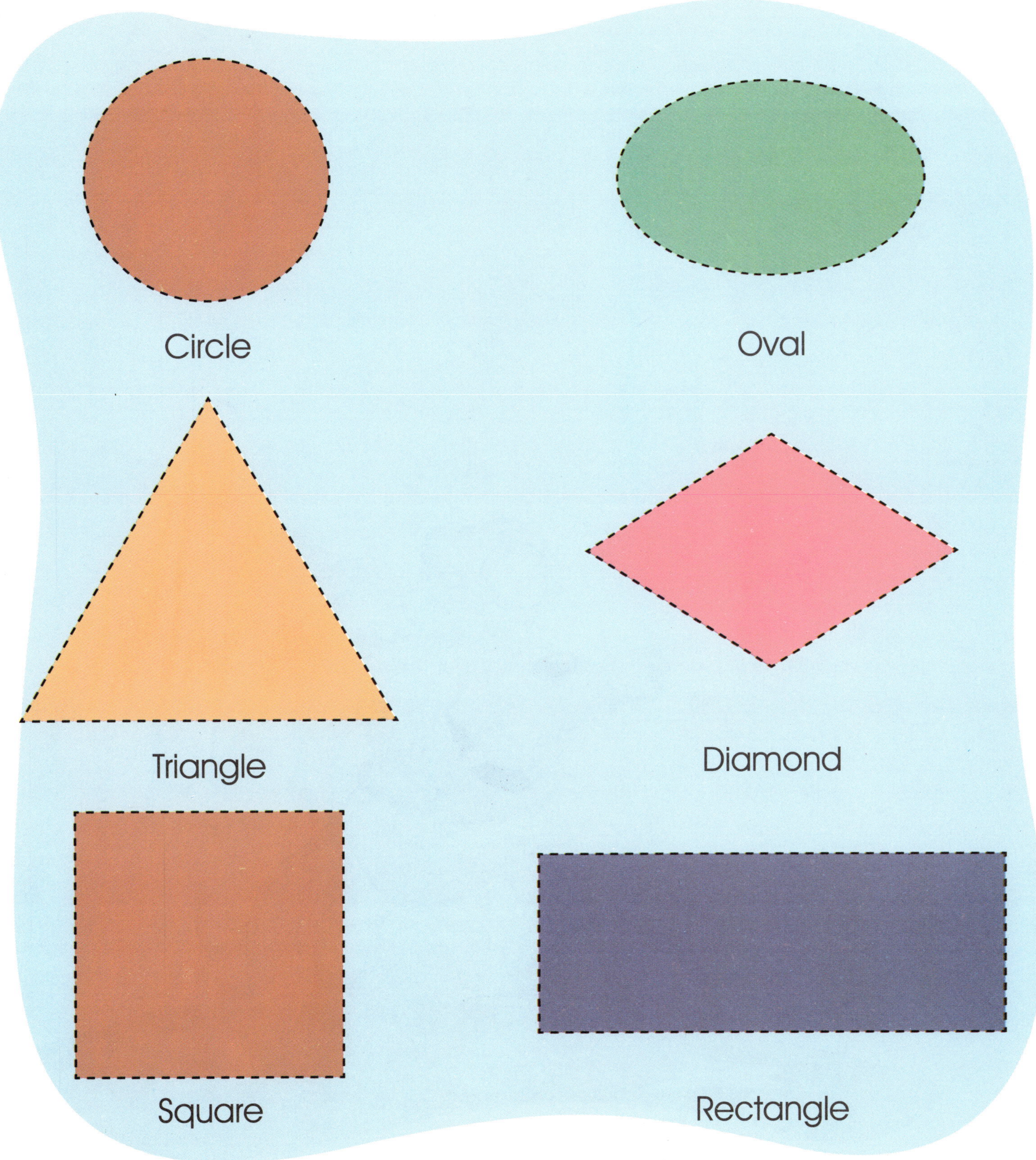

Bubbly Bubbles!

Sandy is playing with bubbles. Trace the circles and colour them.

Knock! Knock!

The eggs are ready to hatch! Trace them. All are oval in shape.

Snack Time!

The ants are hungry! Trace the square chocolates before the ants eat them all.

Let's Go Camping!

The bear is on a camp. Trace and complete the picture.

Fly High!

Help the squirrel fly high with the kites! Trace the diamonds and colour the kites.

Fun with Shapes!

Colour the shapes and count them.

How many did you find? Write the number of each.

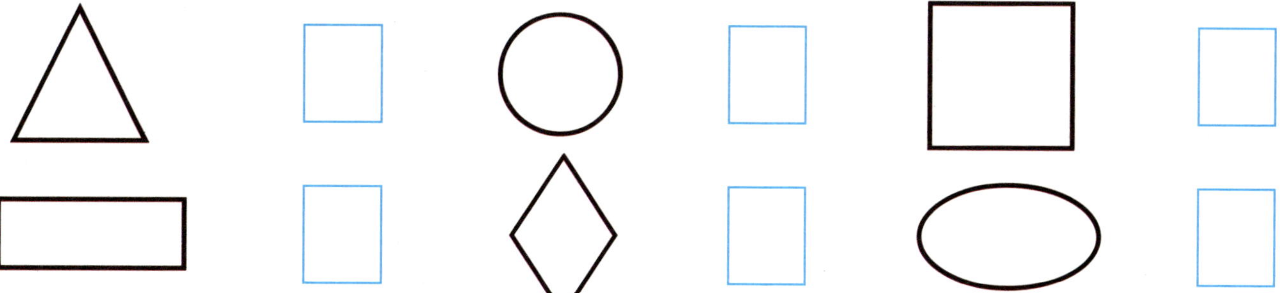

Milk for Sale!

Miss Cow is with her cartons of milk. Trace the rectangles and complete the picture.

Off to the Farm!

Pog is off to the farm. Trace over the dots and complete the picture for him.

Tracing Is Fun!

Welcome the Mud Man! Trace the circles and complete the picture.

Celebration Time!

It's Ronny's birthday! All are ready to celebrate. Trace over the dotted lines and complete the picture.

Up I Climb!

Kim has built a lovely home. Trace all the shapes while he climbs up.

It's Time to Sleep!

Trace over the dots to complete the picture. Then colour it.

Who Is in the Water?

Trace the dotted lines and find out who is swimming in the water. Can you name them?